ANCIENT EGYPTIAN CATS
A Coloring Book
For
Adults and Children

A Great Cat Production

by

L.A. Vocelle

DEDICATION

This book is dedicated to my little love Beseechy Runtus. We will meet again.

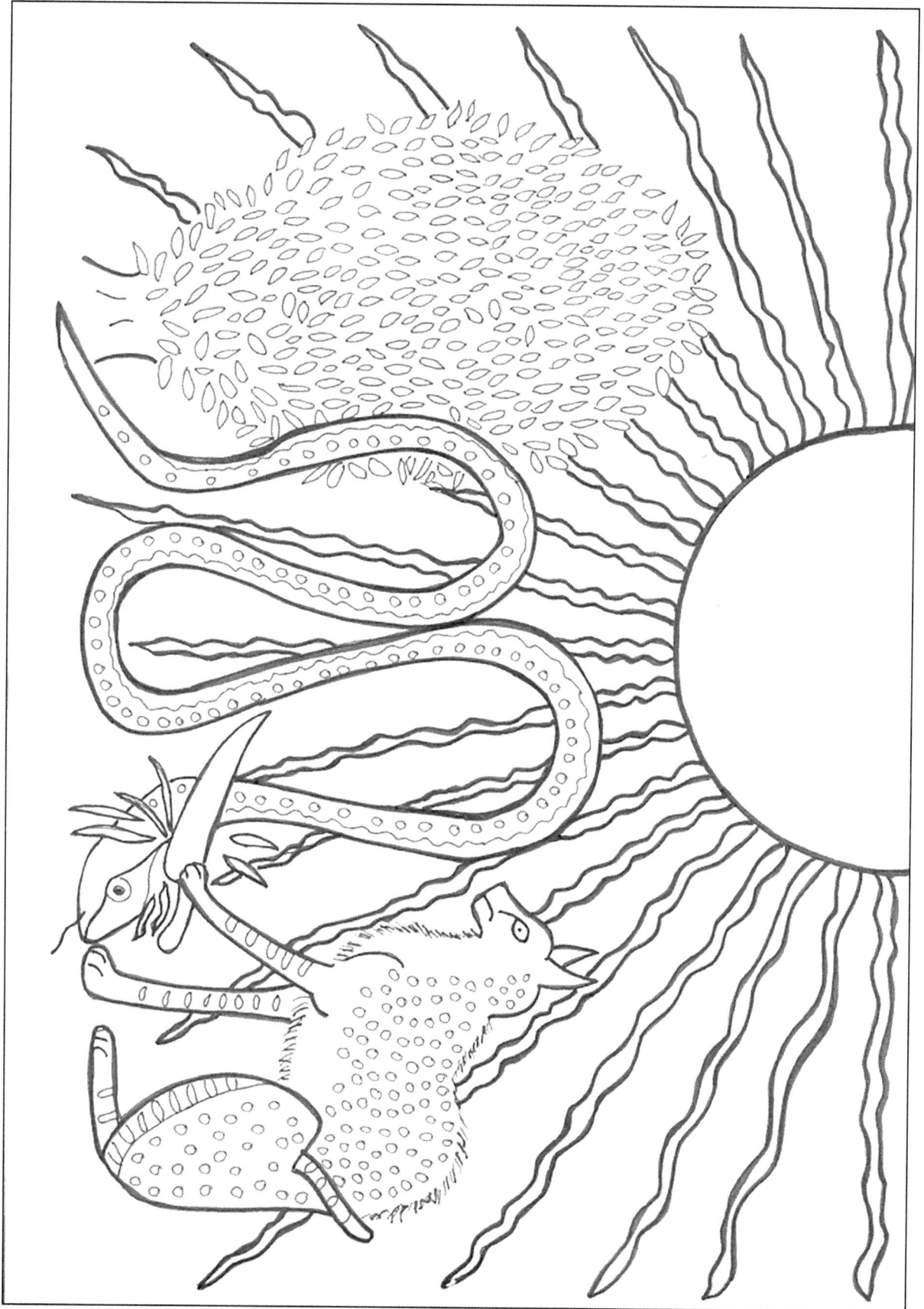

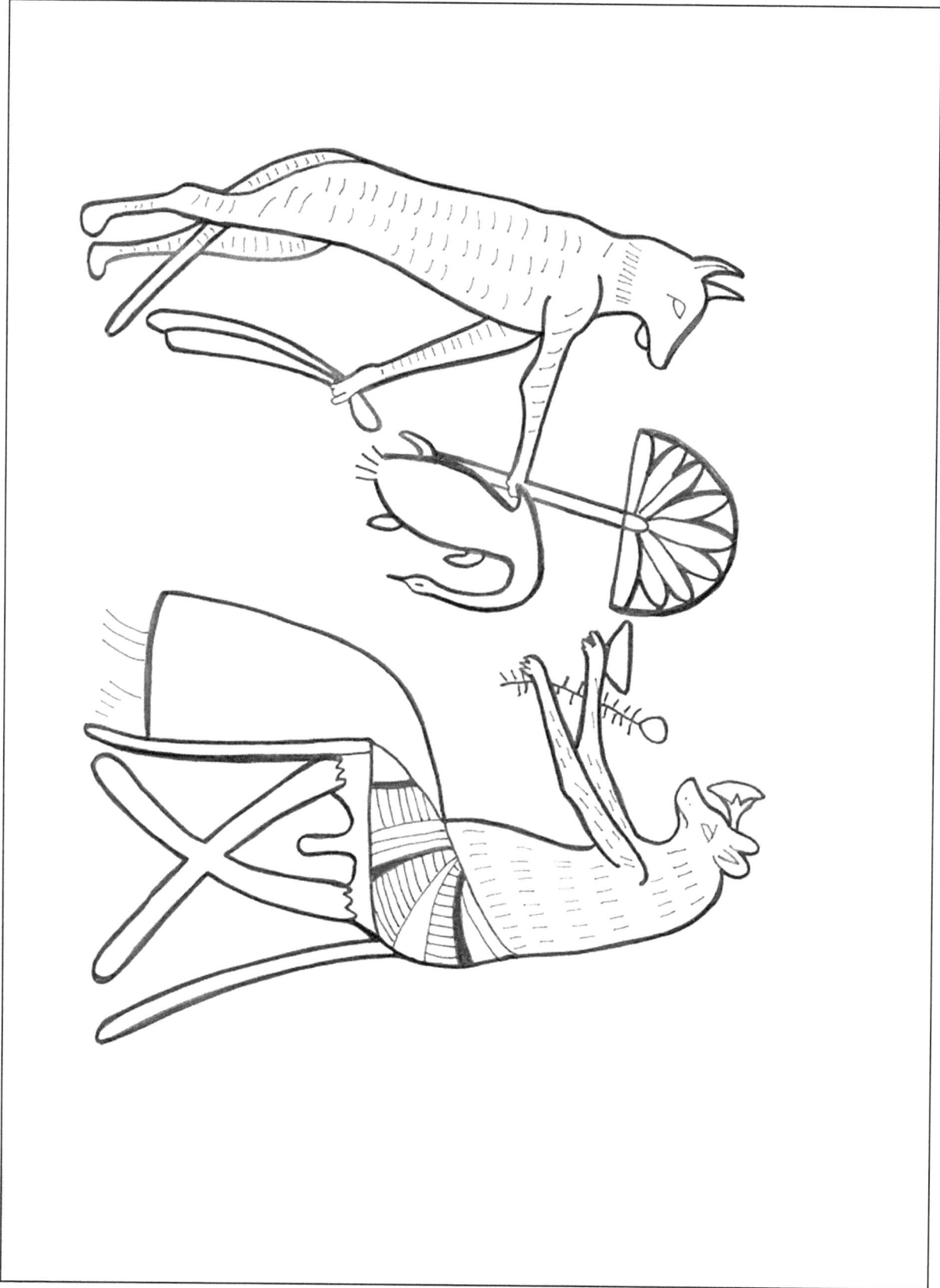

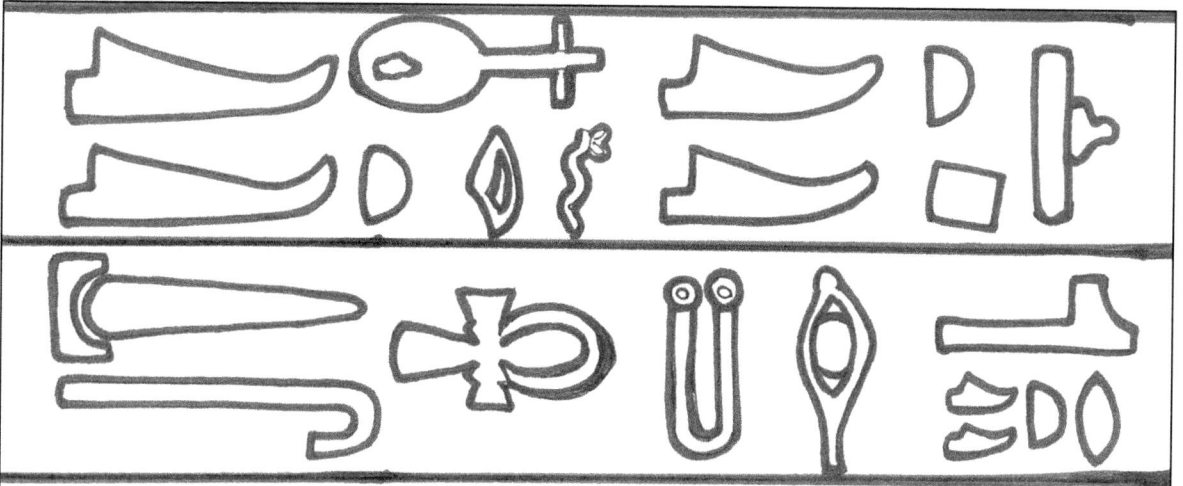

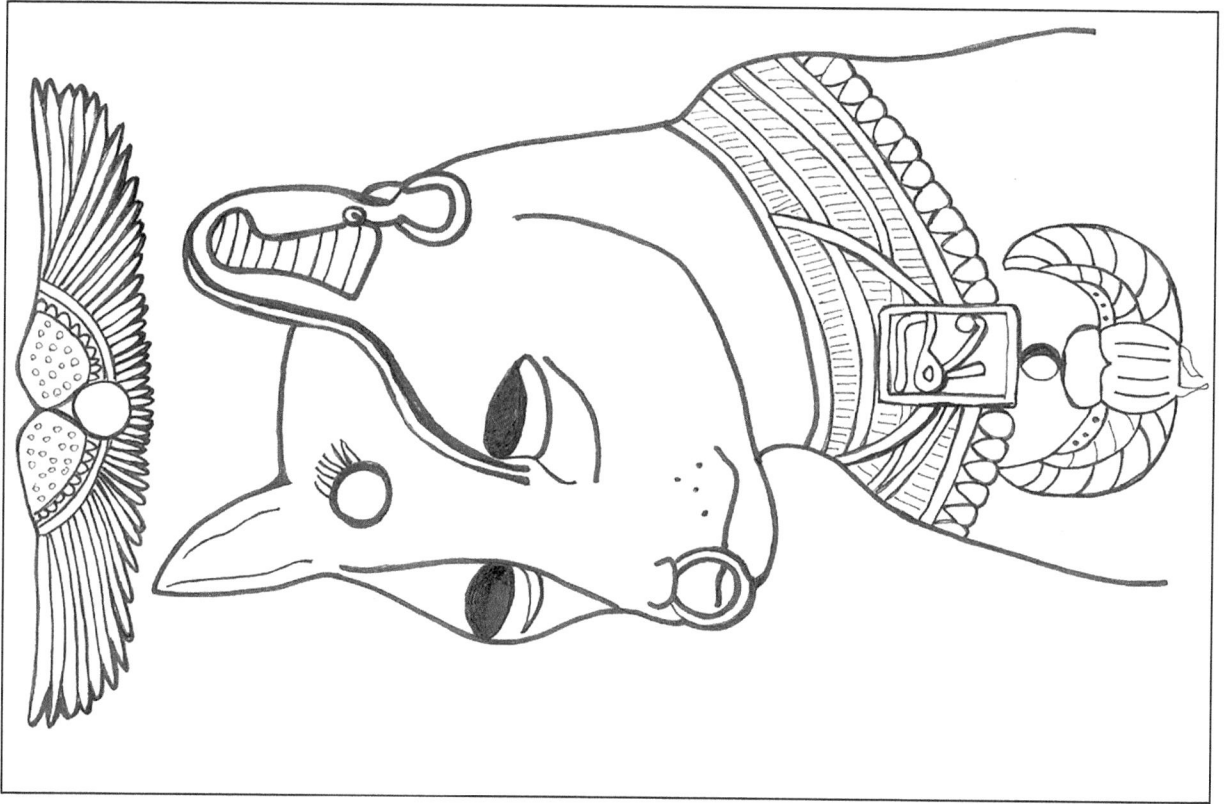

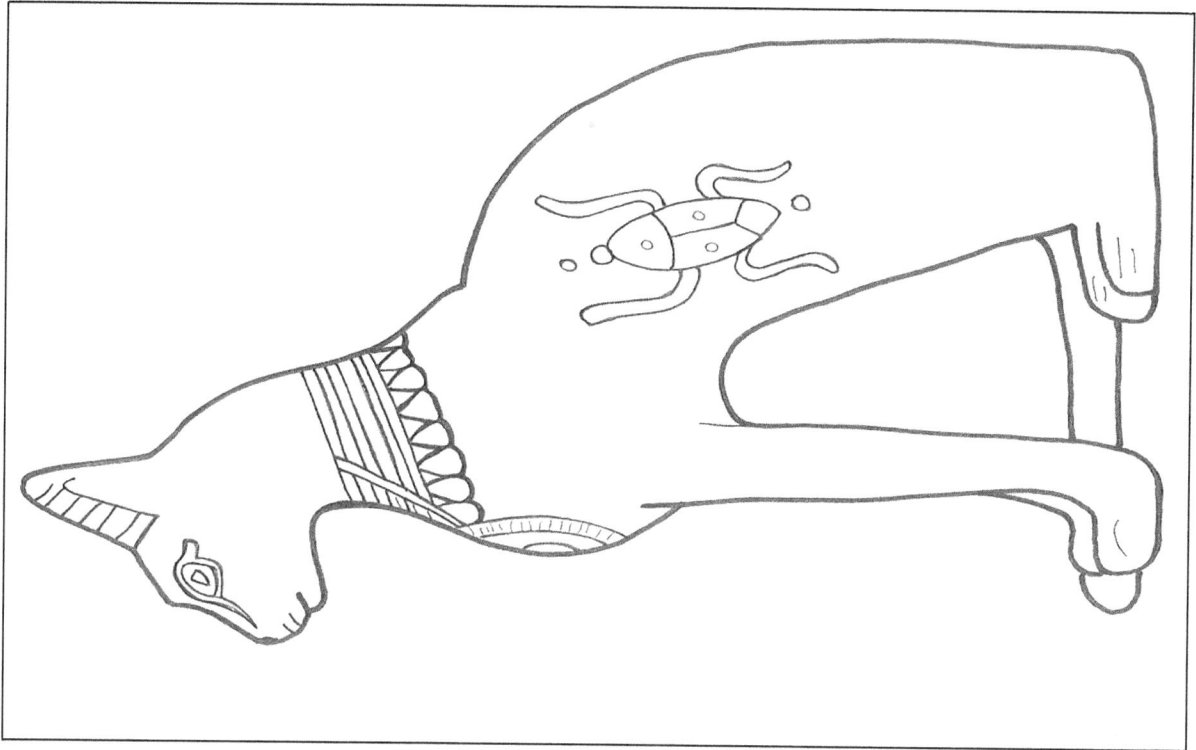

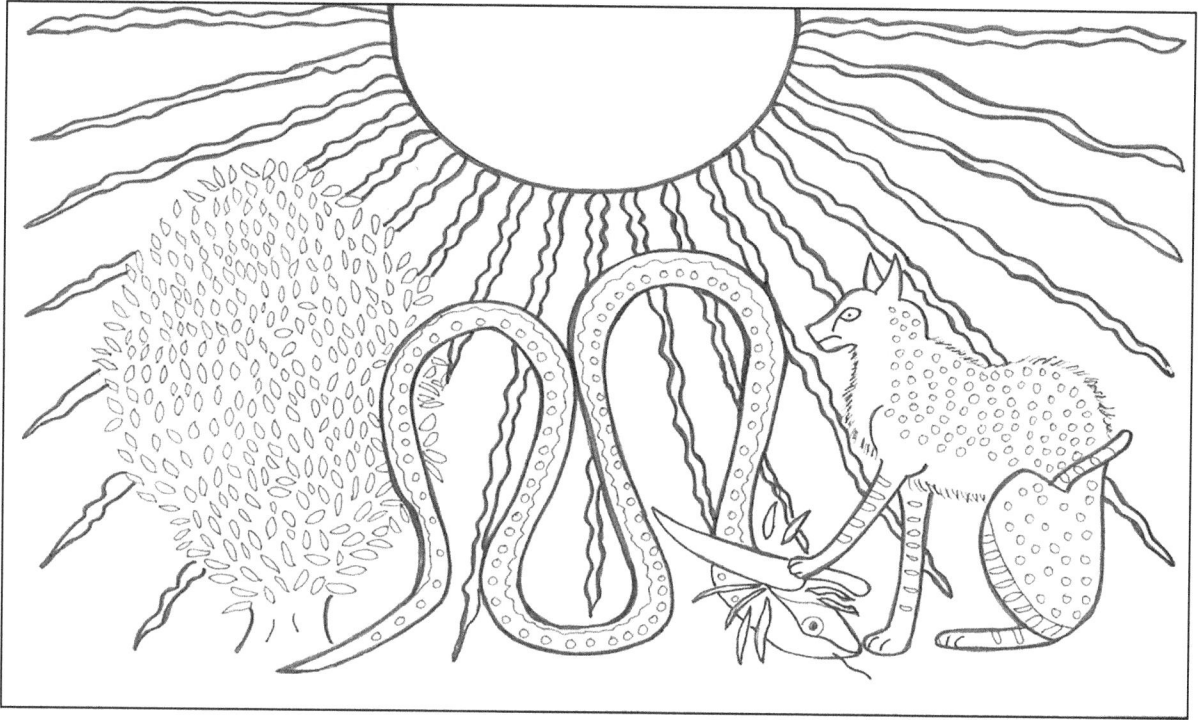

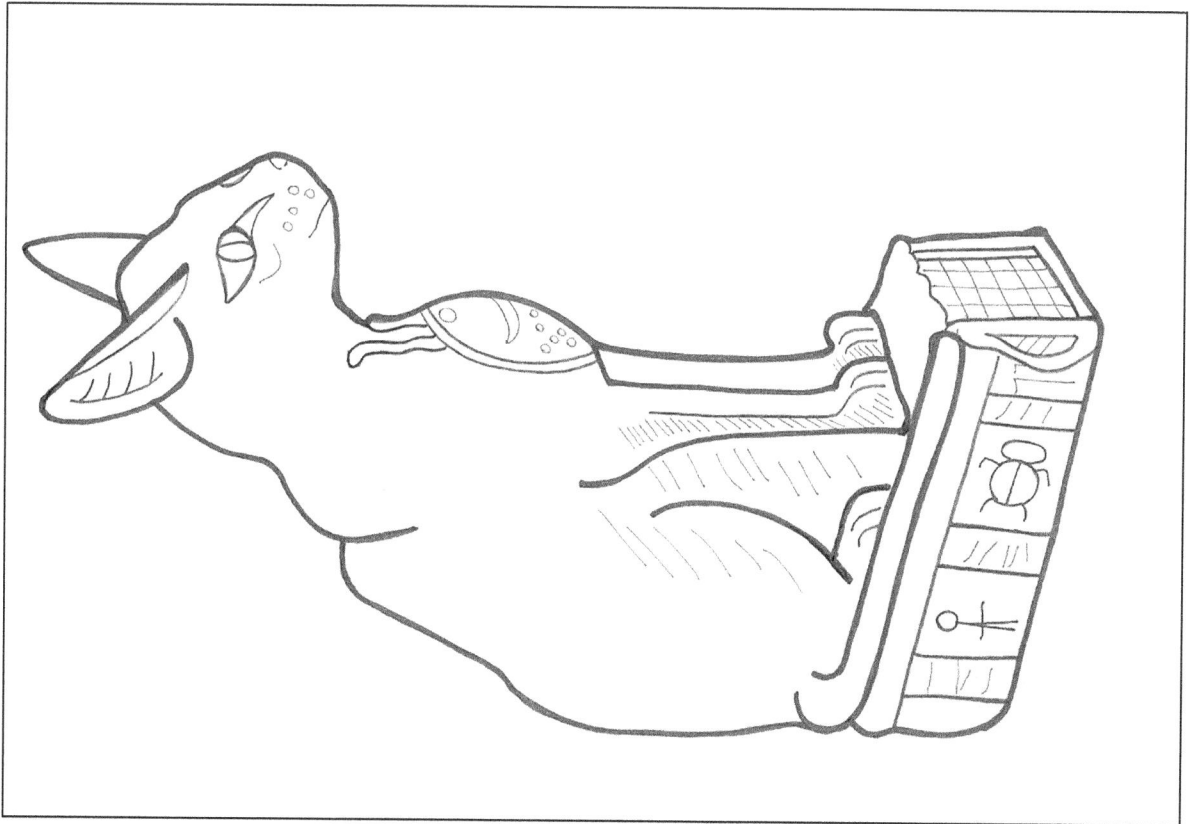

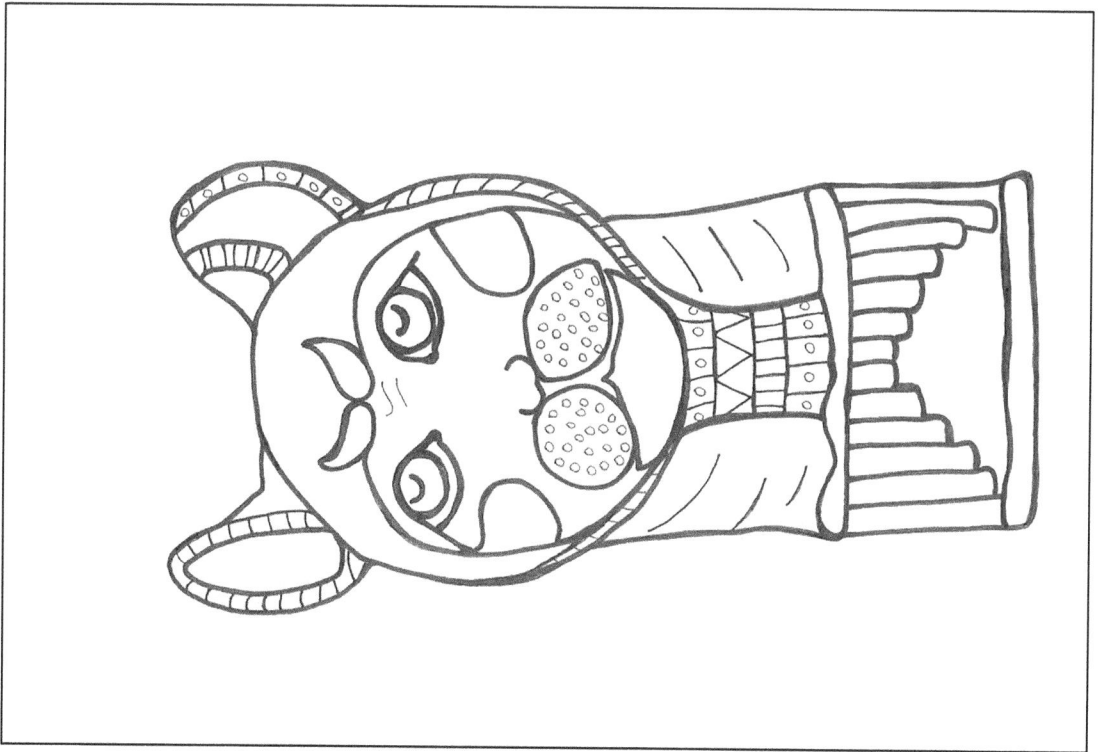

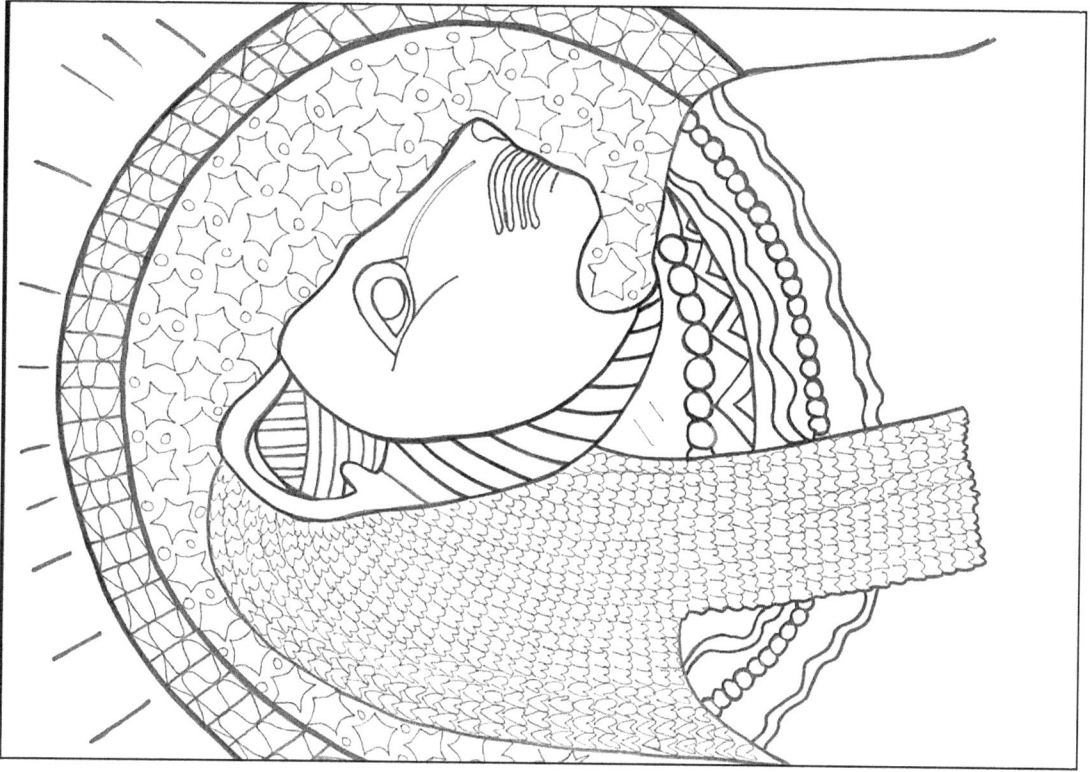
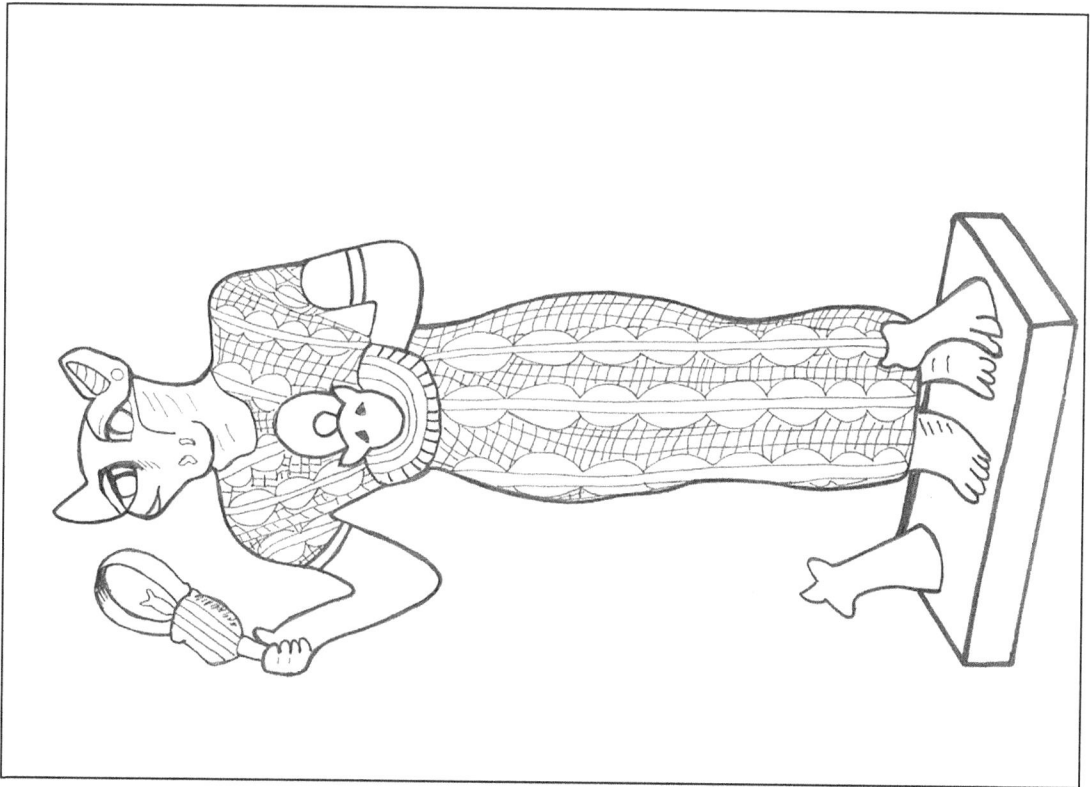

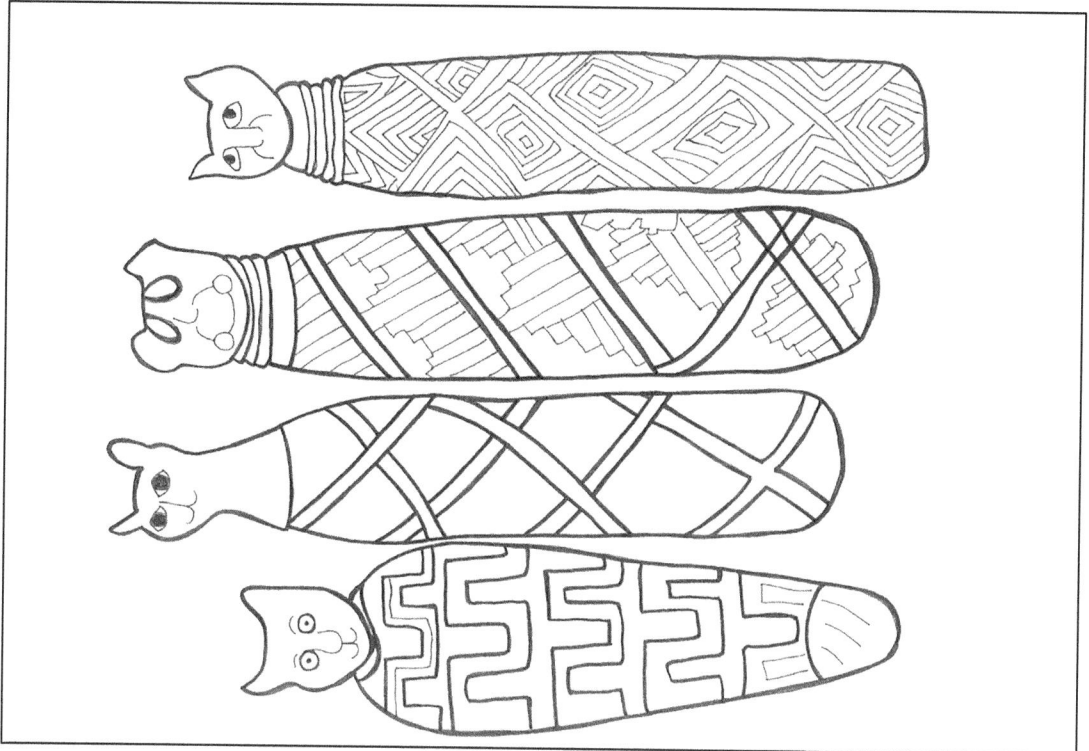

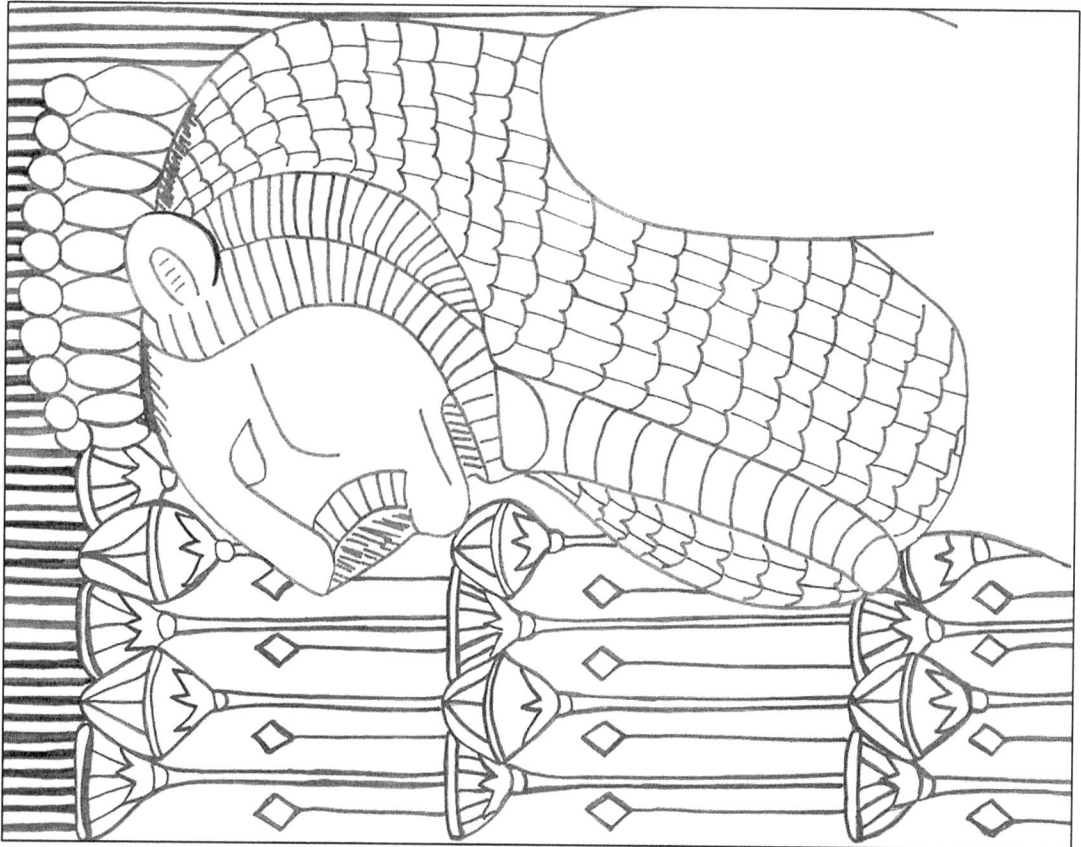

www.ingramcontent.com/pod-product-compliance
Lightning Source LLC
Chambersburg PA
CBHW081546040426
42448CB00015B/3236